Spi-ku

For Jan!
—L. B.

For Aaron, Shana, Devin, and Seth
—R. M.

Published by
PEACHTREE PUBLISHING COMPANY INC.
1700 Chattahoochee Avenue
Atlanta, Georgia 30318-2112
www.peachtree-online.com

Text © 2021 by Leslie Bulion
Illustrations © 2021 by Robert Meganck

Edited by Vicky Holifield
Design and composition by Robert Meganck
Art direction by Adela Pons

The illustrations were rendered digitally.

Printed in November 2020 by Leo Paper Products in China
10 9 8 7 6 5 4 3 2 1 (hardcover)
10 9 8 7 6 5 4 3 2 1 (trade paperback)
First Edition
HC ISBN 978-1-68263-192-8
PB ISBN 978-1-68263-257-4

Cataloging-in-Publication Data is available from the Library of Congress.

Spi-ku

A Clutter of Short Verse on Eight Legs

Written by
Leslie Bulion

Illustrated by
Robert Meganck

PEACHTREE
ATLANTA

Contents

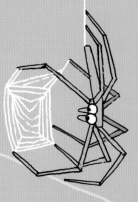

Araneae All Around

From leafy treetop to forest floor,
Where foam-kissed ocean meets shimmery shore,
In boggy wetland and peaceful pond,
Through sand-dry desert and beyond—
We spy spiders!

Hatching from pearly, silk-cocooned eggs,
Stretching eight sensitive, hairy legs,
Tough covers shed as they molt and grow,
Trailing silk draglines wherever they go—
We spy spiders!

Two body parts with a slim connection,
Two jaws poised for venom injection,
An assortment of silks spun from spinnerets
Into egg cases, molting pads, luncheon-nets—
We spy spiders!

Flexible predators, hunting and trapping,
Tricking and dodging and courting and scrapping,
Diving, ballooning, and spitting silk glue,
Come, let's discover what spiders can do—
Let's spy spiders!

(see page 42 for spider
identification)

spiders

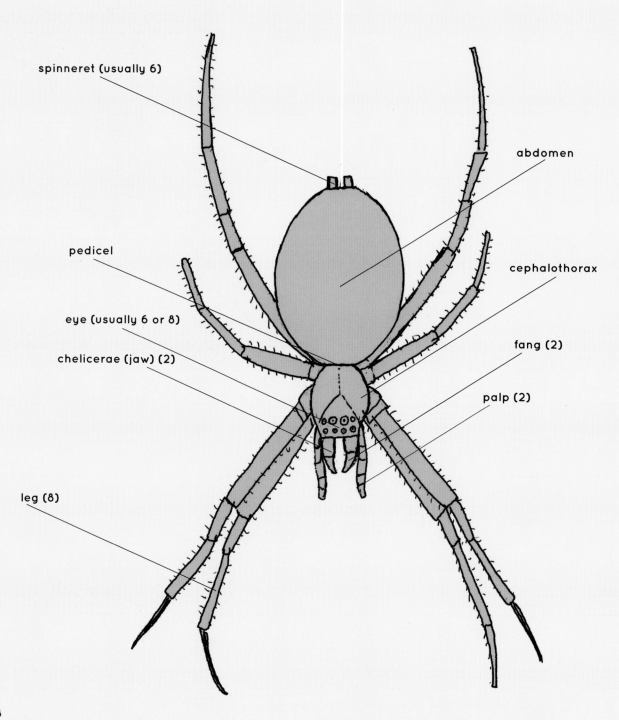

spinneret (usually 6)

abdomen

pedicel

cephalothorax

eye (usually 6 or 8)

fang (2)

chelicerae (jaw) (2)

palp (2)

leg (8)

The World of Spiders

All spiders are arachnids.
But some arachnids
mite not be spiders.

Spiders belong to the class of animals known as arachnids (uh/RACK/nids), along with mites, ticks, scorpions, daddy longlegs, and others. All arachnids have eight legs, a tough and flexible covering called an exoskeleton, and no wings or antennae. All have two main body regions, though some arachnid groups *appear* as if they have just one. Arachnids hatch from eggs looking a lot like they will as adults. As they mature, arachnids shed their exoskeleton several times to make room for their growing body in a process called molting.

Spiders are the only arachnids that have a narrow waist called a pedicel connecting their two main body parts (cephalothorax and abdomen), a venomous bite, *and* spinnerets on their undersides that produce silk. These special traits put them in their own group within the arachnids, the taxonomic order called Araneae (uh/ RAY/nee/ee).

Worldwide, more than forty-eight thousand species of spiders are busy hunting and trapping their prey, which are mostly small invertebrates, including *each other*! Spiders have crawled the Earth for more than 400 million years—plenty of time for these small, fierce predators to evolve their magnificent arsenal of spidery survival skills.

NOT spiders

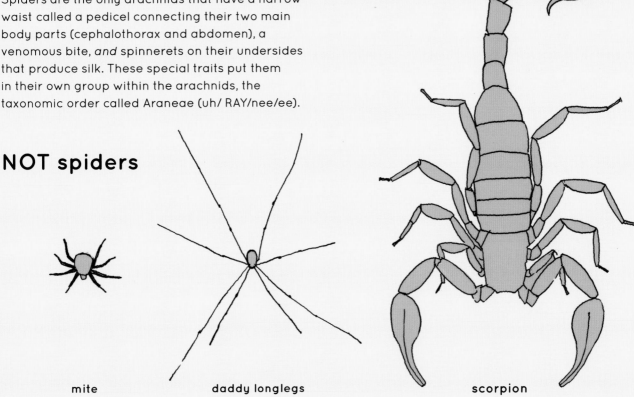

mite   daddy longlegs   scorpion

Golden Silk Orbweaver

sun-shimmer silk
calls six-legged web guests—
dinner!

Spitting Spider

supper hunter
lumbers in the dark
no speed needed
when fangs spray sticky zigzags
of prey-pinning silk

Spectacular Silk

A spider uses its feet to pull stretchy silk threads from spigots called spinnerets at the end of its abdomen. Many spiders can add gluey droplets to make their silk sticky. Others comb special wooly catching threads from an organ called the cribellum (crih/BELL/um) on their underside, in front of their spinnerets.

All spiders spin at least two kinds of silk. But fewer than half of known spider species weave prey-trapping webs. The **golden silk orbweaver** is one of many orbweavers that trap prey in classic spokes-and-spiral webs.

Spitting spiders are able to fire a gluey, venomous liquid silk from their fangs to pin and trap prey.

Spiders also use silk to wrap prey, weave egg sacs, or line burrows. A spider on the move plays out a silk safety thread, occasionally anchoring it along its path with a silken staple. When danger threatens, the spider bungees away on this dragline to a soft landing—hopefully in a predator-free zone!

Tarantulas like this **desert blond tarantula** and some other large spiders weave silk pads to lie on with their legs in the air when they molt.

Desert Blond Tarantula

comfy
on her silk pad
tarantula bursts her
tight exoskeleton and splits—
all's swell!

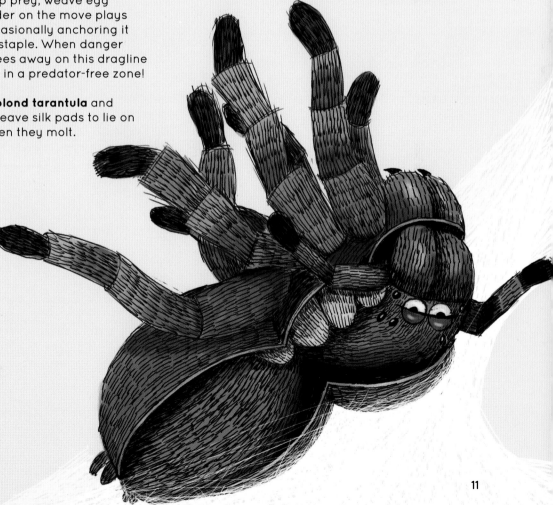

Spiders on the Move

When a spider walks, it lifts four legs at a time. First, the spider might lift the first and third legs on its right side along with the second and fourth legs on its left side. Next, those four legs stay put while the spider lifts its second and fourth legs on its right side plus the first and third legs on its left. A spider's legs are all attached to its first body part, the cephalothorax (SEH/fuh/low/THAW/racks).

To bend its legs, a spider contracts (shortens) its muscles. To straighten its legs, a spider increases blood flow into them, creating pressure against its exoskeleton. A sudden rush of blood into the rear legs of jumping spiders helps these acrobats leap more than twenty-five times their own height—*BOING!*

Some spiders can walk on the water's surface without sinking. **Fishing spiders** can also row, using their second and third pairs of legs like oars, or raise their first pair of legs and sail across the water. Certain fishing and wolf spiders and the diving bell spider can dive and crawl *under* water!

Many spiderlings and even some adult spiders let fly fine silk threads, ballooning into morning breezes to find a new home. Scientists have shown that electrical charges in spider silk can push spiders away from the Earth and pull them up toward the sky. For some spiders, a watery touchdown is their unfortunate end. But others, such as the **common stretch spider**, can raise their front legs or abdomens to catch air with their "sails."

For a speedy getaway from the predatory spider wasp's sting and egg deposit, the **golden wheel spider** flips onto its side, tucks its legs, and cartwheels down the steep sand dunes of its desert home. *Whee!*

Fishing Spider

Row, row, row my legs,
Pairs two and three are oars,
My first legs feel the way ahead,
Which do no work? My fours!

Spider Ballooning

up on eight tiptoes
gossamer silk streamers
many flying kites

some aeronauts
in unplanned splashdown
windsurf

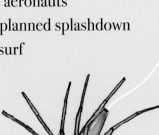

Golden Wheel Spider

She'd sting me, then sting-in her egg,
That spider wasp on host patrol,
But I'm no hatching wasp's first meal,
Look—I'm a wheel! *That's* how I roll!

Food Prep, Mealtime, Leftovers

Most spiders hunt or trap many kinds of prey, including insects, other small invertebrates, and plenty of their spider neighbors. Some haul in bigger catch such as fish, amphibians, or even the occasional hatchling bird. Though a few add plant nectar to their diet, spiders must enjoy *all* of their delicious foods in liquid form. How do they do it?

Nearly all spiders paralyze or kill prey with a venomous bite from sharp-fanged jaws called chelicerae (cheh/LIH/suh/ray). Most also wrap their prey in silk. Some spiders bite first, injecting venom before they wrap, while others pin or wrap first, *then* bite. Some change strategies if their prey might harm *them*. The hackled orbweavers are a family of spiders that have lost their ability to make venom, and instead simply crush their prey into small packages, using lots and lots of silk wrapping.

All spiders drool digestive juices into their prey. These juices convert their victim's soft insides into a slurpable, nutritious feast. Most spiders use their jaws to crunch while they drool. Then they suck up liquefied critter, leaving a heap of exoskeleton bits. Crab spiders and comb-footed spiders don't have crunching jaws, so they drool-and-drink, drool-and-drink, leaving an empty insect container behind.

Though they are quite successful at "liquidating" their prey, nearly all spiders will try to hide or run away to avoid an encounter with us. Most have chelicerae that are too weak to bite into human skin. And very few species have venom powerful enough to cause humans serious harm.

Spider Munchtime

Wrap bite *blergh*
SLURRRP.
Bite wrap *blergh* chew
SLURRRP.
B-i-i-i-i-i-te...*blergh*
SLURRRP.
Wrap (crush/smother) *blergh*
SLURRRP.

Each spider
uses its own family recipe
to make a fly smoothie.

(see page 42 for spider identification)

15

Worldwide Webbers

Each species of sit-and-wait web spider strings its own type of tricky trap. Spiders weave prey-catching webs in rounded orbs, flat sheets, funnels, triangles, ladders, tubes, and more. A tangled cobweb may look messy, but its catching threads turn pesky insects like mosquitoes and gnats into spider fodder. Male web spiders spend most of their short adult lives finding mates instead of weaving webs.

Orbweavers like the **black-and-yellow garden spider** spin sticky spiral wheels across dry silk spokes. Many decorate their webs with wooly silk decorations called stabilimenta (STAY/bil/ih/MEN/tuh) that may disguise the spider on her web or warn birds not to fly through. Some of these decorations even attract insect prey *into* the web.

The **ogre-faced spider** holds a tiny web net between her four bent front legs. When she sees movement, she straightens her legs, trapping prey with her silken net—*gotcha!*

The **ray orbweaver** weaves a web consisting of dry silk threads stretched across a river. Shorter, sticky threads hang down from the dry silk cross threads to touch the water's surface. When a surface-skimming insect bumps one of her sticky fishing lines, this spider reels in a meal.

Black-and-Yellow Garden Spider

An orbweaver called it a night,
Belly stuffed in the dusk's waning light.
Then a hurrying fly
Crashed her web and stuck by,
And the spider shrugged, "Well...*one* more bite."

Ogre-faced Spider

upside-down ready
tremendous eyes scan the dark
motion detected
snap open leg-net—*bagged it!*
(food never sees me coming)

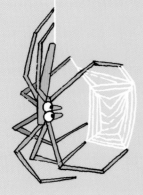

Ray Orbweaver

Hung from dry silk rays that span a river,
Down to water's surface, holding fast,
Sticky threads that trap and then deliver,
Water strider dinner skimming past.

On the Prowl

Half of all known spider species capture prey without using webs or snares. These hunters actively stalk prey, sit and wait for prey to come within pouncing range, or hide to ambush their meal. Many are nocturnal and some hunt by day. Most will take an assortment of prey.

The **goldenrod crab spider** is a daytime ambusher whose flat shape and color-changing talent help it hide in plain sight. Sitting motionless on a matching flower, the crab spider waits for a pollinator to fly in for a snack.

The **woodlouse hunter** has curved fangs built to grab and pierce the tough exoskeletons of nighttime crawlers like millipedes and woodlice. Woodlice are known by many names, including sowbugs, pillbugs, or roly-polies.

The **diving bell spider** is the only spider able to _live_ underwater. To manage this, it weaves a silken dome in an underwater plant and fills the dome with air collected at the surface. The spider darts out of this diving bell to grab a small swimming meal, delivers a venomous bite, and returns home to feed.

Goldenrod Crab Spider

My strong venom bite
knocks the fight from a bee.
Yikes!
The knockout's too slow.
Can't let go!
Wait...whoa...
> _WHEEE!_

Woodlouse Hunter

Stalking by feel
in the dark is ideal
when it ends in a meal.

Diving Bell Spider

scuba spider
wears a silver bubble
dines in

Bolas Spider

My swinging string is armed with glue
(A gob of moth-adhesive goo).
These hopeful males don't have a clue,
Their destiny is spider stew.
By day, I rest in open view,
A shapely splat of birdy-poo.

Spider Foolery

Spiders are impostors who use chemical scents, movement, shape, and color to fool prey *and* predators. Their disguises bring prey within striking range and keep predators from recognizing spiders as foodstuff.

The **bolas spider** attracts male moths by making a chemical that smells like *female* moths. As male moths arrive on the scene, the spider weaves a bola-shaped "web," which is simply a single thread with a sticky blob on its end. If a male moth flies in close enough—*WHAP!*—suppertime for spider! By day the lumpy bolas spider passes for an unappetizing bird-dropping.

Ant-mimics are ant-shaped spiders. They look like ants but walk like spiders. When they stand still, they wave their first or second pair of legs in the air like ants' antennae. Since ants often taste bad or fight back, would-be predators look elsewhere for an easier meal.

One ant-mimic, the **green ant-hunter spider**, sports an additional disguise: ant perfume. Giving off the ants' own chemical scent allows this jumping spider to swipe green tree ant larvae (newly hatched young) from the jaws of their worker ant caregivers *without being attacked*—a bold trick!

The smile on the abdomen of the **Hawaiian happy-face spider** is only one of that species' many color patterns. Scientists studying this species think its range of markings may confuse bird predators. When birds hesitate, these spiders are happy to escape!

Green Ant-Hunter Spider

2 SPIDER · LEG SPIDER · LEG · SPIDER · LEG · 1 SPIDER · LEG SPIDER · LEG · PALP · PALP · SPIDER · SPIDER · SPIDER · SPIDER · LEG · SPIDER · SPIDER · 3 LEG · LEG 4 · SPIDER · SPIDER · SPIDER · LEG 5 · LEG 6 · SPIDER LEG · SPIDER · LEG SPIDER · SPIDER · SPIDER · LEG 8 · LEG 7

pretender stops
waves front legs as "ANTennae"
predator moves on

NOT
ANT

eight-legger enters
cloaked in ant colony's scent
news flash: LARVAE HEIST!

Hawaiian Happy-Face Spiders

They're marked
with smiles
or with
    a frown,
they're often yellow,
sometimes brown
with spotty dots,
    or blots
      of red,
variety
may help them flee,
quite happily
    alive
    not dead.

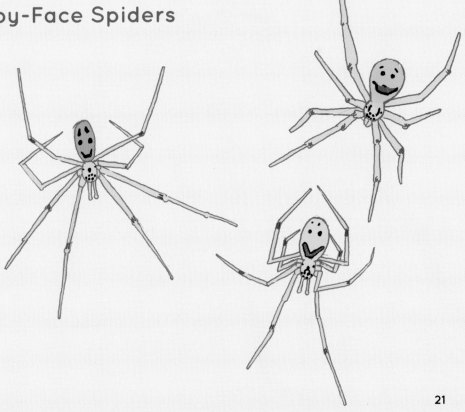

Spidey Senses

Spiders' exoskeletons are covered with tiny hairs and narrow slits that sense vibrations in the air and under*feet*, giving spiders detailed information about their environment. Spiders receive mealtime messages along silk threads from insects trapped far across the web. Special slits in their exoskeletons also give spiders information about their position—like a spider GPS.

Spiders "smell" using sensory hairs to detect chemicals in the air. Other sensory hairs allow spiders to "taste" by touching with their front legs and palps (short appendages next to their chelicerae) as they walk. The male **tiger wandering spider** follows a female's trail by touch-tasting her silk dragline.

Most spiders rely on chemical messages and vibrations since they have relatively weak eyesight. But daytime hunters like the **white-mustached portia** and other jumping spiders use their eight keen eyes to identify and pinpoint prey, measure attack distance, and *POUNCE!*

Instead of weaving a web, a **twig-lining trapdoor spider** attaches a fan of twigs, leaves, or grass to its burrow's camouflaged trapdoor. Then it hides underneath with its foot touching the door's underside or an attached twig. The spider waits for a vibration. When an unsuspecting ant or beetle jostles the booby-trapped door, the spider pops out—*surprise!*

Tiger Wandering Spider

touch...taste...follow...
her perfumed silk trail invites
a wandering mate

White-Mustached Portia

I eat my spider cousins. Yes. That's right.
I see them, track them, JUMP, then power-bite.

To sidestep spitting spider's silk attack,
I take the slow approach, behind its back.

When spitter's jaws hold eggs and she can't shoot,
I see I'm free to take the head-on route.

Twig-Lining Trapdoor Spiders

These bulky, burrowing, trap-setter spiders
Are crafty, underflap hiders.

Their doorbells of fanned-out twigs mark the spot
Where ants may meander, then *(flip! grab!)* may not.

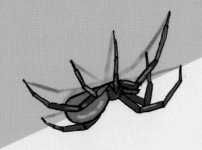

Southern House Spider

giving up
one pudgy velvet leg—
no problem

seven-legged escape
leaves predator holding
a tasty morsel

Longbodied Cellar Spider

hungry wasp
knob-kneed arachnid
a whirling blur
invisibility cloak—
cobweb to be continued...

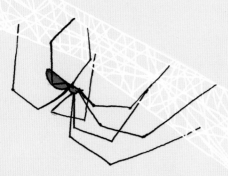

Don't Feed the Spider-Eaters!

For most spiders, the best defense against enemies involves hiding—either in burrows and crevices or camouflaged in plain sight. Out in the open, spiders drop on draglines, run away, or crumple their legs to play dead.

If an attacker grabs a spider's leg, most spiders can let that leg disconnect from their body to get away as the **southern house spider** does. If the spider is young and has not yet molted into its final adult exoskeleton, it will usually grow a replacement leg. Adults that have finished molting will manage their spidery lives on seven legs, or even on only six.

A **longbodied cellar spider** clings to its corner cobweb, vibrating into a hard-to-grab blur when it senses a wasp or other predator nearby.

Some spiders stand their ground and flash fangs, leak stinky fluid, spit venom, or fling silk in the face of an attacker. Some will bite. A threatened **Goliath bird-eating spider** can rub its legs together to make a snakelike hiss. If a predator closes in, this tarantula rubs its abdomen and lets loose a choking cloud of tiny, irritating hairs.

Goliath Bird-Eating Spider

My name is Goliath.
I *am* big.
But I don't eat birds.
They try to munch *me*.
Hey, birds: eat my dust!
See? I'm no bird-eater.
Wait...
does the rare hatchling chick count?

Tricky Spider Enemies (part 1)

Spiders face a wide assortment of trickster critters (including other spiders) that try to steal spidery handiwork, such as their carefully wrapped prey, their silk, or their protein-packed bodies.

While many birds eat spiders, **hummingbirds** help themselves to *prey* trapped in spiders' webs. A hummingbird may also steal the fluffy silk some spiders (such as this **featherlegged orbweaver**) spin; they'll use it to line their soft, stretchy nest cup. Some hummingbirds may use the silk to help leaf and lichen camouflage cling to their nest's outer side.

The Featherlegged Orbweaver **and** the Hummingbird

Now where's that gnat
I caught today?

I stole it,
zip-flit!
Flew away.
And now I'm back
for silky fluff,
your wooly, catchy, stretchy
                          stuff,
to make my cup nest
snug enough.

But I don't trap and spin for *you*—
That's how I make *my* living!

TOUGH!

Tricky Spider Enemies (part 2)

Wasps eat spiders and may deliver spider take-out to their nest of wormy wasp larvae. Some wasps lay eggs onto or into spiders' bodies, providing a ready buffet for hatching larvae to live as spider parasites. One wormy **wasp larva** lives *on* the spider's abdomen and makes a chemical that forces its **orbweaver** host to spin a strange, strong web. The wasp larva attaches its cocoon to this platform web, then metamorphoses into a flying adult wasp.

The Orbweaver **and** The Wasp Larva

I'm pierced!

Get out!

I guess you'll stay.

Wait—what'd you say?
And why's my weaving
gone astray?

My web looks weird...

You're good.

I would,
but you're my host.

I'll have the
spider blood buffet.

*(My potion's in!
Now you'll obey.)*

Nothing's amiss—
it's set for
metamorphosis.
I'll drink up now.
Ta-da!
Kiss! Kiss!

Tricky Spider Enemies (part 3)

Pirate spiders strum the threads of other spiders' webs, playing that spider's mating tune, or the tune of trapped prey. These vibrations lure the other spider—even a **southern black widow**—to come within striking distance.

The Pirate Spider and the Southern Black Widow

I'll creep so she
won't notice
me

I'll trim her web threads so she
won't reach
me

I'll pluck the fly tune so she
won't know
me

Sounds like dinner.
Hmm...I'll go see.
Who bit my leg?

Yo-ho!
It's me!

Spider Comes A-Courting

Since spiders often devour each other, a male will send special signals to a female to let her know he wants to mate—*not* be on the menu! If she accepts his advances, he'll give her a packet of sperm to store, which she'll use to fertilize her eggs. If she's not interested, he'd better make a quick getaway... *or else!*

Many male spiders use sounds or vibrations to send mating signals. They "drum" against the ground, shake, or rub a leg across comblike bumps on their bodies. Some spiders strum a special mating "tune" on the female's web. But even after the poor **redback spider** shakes, strums, then mates with a female, he's *still* likely to be her supper!

Since spiders that hunt by day have excellent eyesight, these courting males use signals females will *see*, such as waving fancy-shaped feet or dancing a spider two-step. A male **peacock spider** raises, expands, and shakes his brightly colored abdomen like a flag to say, "Pick me!"

Some male **nursery web spiders** distract mates with a freshly wrapped insect gift. But even if a male spider manages to survive the perils of courtship and mating, his life ends shortly afterward. And once he dies, his body is likely to become a meal for some*body* else!

Redback Spider

I played your tune
beneath the moon
I strummed
and your web *hummmmmmed.*

Now I'll creep near,
Hello, my dear.
You like me? Great!
I'm your winning mate!
Ouch! Wait...

This is my fate?
Your spitty, poisoned chew-and-bite?
So cannibal-like! So impolite!

Peacock Spider Hoe-Down

Spider gal, won't you come out today?
I'll wave my legs,
Skitter, sashay.
Spider gal, won't you give me a sign,
And we'll dance by the light of the sun!

Spider gal, I'll flip up my flap,
With bold designs,
I'm a flashy chap!
Spider gal, won't you signal you're mine,
And we'll dance by the light of the sun!

Nursery Web Spider

I've brought a gift. See? I'm well-bred!
I'll stand, front legs above my head,
If you attack me I'll play dead.
Here—
        eat this silk-wrapped fly, instead!

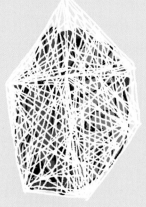

Spiny Orbweaver Cocoon

wrapped in a dead leaf
an egg-filled fluffball becomes
forest litter

Spider Mamas

Some tiny female spiders lay fewer than ten eggs at a time, while larger spiders may lay up *to one thousand* eggs or more. Spider mothers protect their eggs in soft, silken cocoons.

Web weavers provide little care beyond camouflaging or tucking away their cocoons. The **spiny orbweaver** binds her cocoon in a dead leaf and lowers it to the forest floor. After the cocoon's snug landing, the parenting duties—and *life*—of this web mama come to an end.

Unlike web weavers, hunting spiders protect their cocoons until hatching time and may carry cocoons in their jaws or attached to their spinnerets. The **dock spider** belongs to a group of spiders called nursery web spiders. These hunters surround their cocoons with silken tents and stand guard until hatchlings leave the nursery tents to find their own spidery hunting grounds.

Some species of spider moms provide more parental care, offering wrapped insects to their growing brood. Others spit up pre-digested, liquid food or lay extra eggs to feed hungry hatchlings. Instead of waiting to be fed, **Australian social crab spider** youngsters pierce Mama's leg joints and help themselves to her deliciously nutritious blood!

Dock Spider Eggs

In Mama's jaws, we take a ride,
She suns us warm, she dunks us damp,
She weaves a tent, we're safe inside,
A thousand eggs at spider camp!

We hatch, and Mama still stands guard,
Until we molt and wander on,
No fond goodbyes for Mom—that's hard,
Just empty spider skins. We're *gone!*

Australian Social Crab Spiderlings

Our home-sweet-nest's a mess, not neat,
A eucalyptus leaf retreat,
Where Mom brings bugs we love to eat.

When frost kills Mom's deliveries
In fall, we drink blood from her knees,
She gives her all, she lives to please,
Which does her in, by small degrees.

Spiders in SpiderTown

Group living helps many animals avoid predators, catch prey, and raise young. But most spiders don't play nicely with others—even their own families! Of the more than forty-eight thousand known spider species, scientists have found fewer than ninety species living in groups.

Australian social huntsman spiders cooperate by sharing some of the work in a family of up to three hundred flat-bodied spiders. Mothers defend the family's hideaway (tucked beneath the bark of a dead tree) against predators. Older brothers and sisters hunt by night, dropping partially eaten prey back home where younger spiderlings polish it off.

Many group-living spiders share space, but the spiders don't cooperate. Each **Mexican colonial orbweaver** strings its own web in a frame shared with fifty to several thousand neighbors. When one spider suddenly drops on its dragline, others recognize the warning: *predator*. Fully grown spiders weave their webs in the center of the group where fewer prey insects land, but insects that do make it to the center are bigger, juicier bugs that didn't stick to an outer web and bounced in. *Score!*

South American social spiders have been observed living in groups as large as fifty thousand! These red, pencil eraser–sized cobweb weavers create a tree-covering, communal web. Working together they will overpower prey as large as a grasshopper. Mother spiders share childcare, barfing up pre-eaten insects to feed any mama's hungry hatchlings.

Australian Social Huntsman Tweens

Our tiny spiderling sisters and brothers,
Tuck in at home with our huntsman mothers.
We're the night predators, swift-crawling, thin-ish,
We bring home leftovers (*if* we can't finish).

Mexican Colonial Orbweaver

large spiders weave center webs
small ones' webs ring the edges
where prey drop in frequently
as do predators

South American Social Spiders

Females spin spirals,
Males crisscross, until
leafy spaces fill,
twigs and limbs drape,
in an immense, tangled, silken cape
few rainforest flitterers
will likely
escape.

Appreciate Araneae!

Silkishly, creepishly,
Eight-legged predators
Toil, never getting
The thanks they are due.

Spiders eat pests set to
Sting, bite, and crop-munch—
They liquidate critters that
Live to bug YOU!

Our Spiderful World

Spiders are small, beautifully efficient hunters and trappers found in every habitat except the open ocean and Antarctica. Without spider predators, populations of their prey would explode—including disease carriers such as mosquitoes and flies, as well as pests that devour our wild plants and cultivated crops. When we humans protect Earth's clean air, soil, water, and open spaces, spiders can keep doing their important ecosystem job that helps *us*.

Thank you for your carnivorously
good work, spider friends!

(see page 43 for spider
identification)

Glossary

abdomen—the second part of a spider's body containing the heart, gut, reproductive system, air exchange system, and silk glands

arachnid—the taxonomic class of animals with eight legs, an outer skeleton, two main body parts, and no wings or antennae; spiders, ticks, mites, scorpions, whip scorpions, harvestmen, and others

araneae—spiders; the taxonomic order of arachnids having a venomous bite, silk-producing spinnerets, and a narrow stalk between the two body parts

carnivore—an animal that eats other animals

cephalothorax—the first part of a spider's body containing sensory organs, feeding structures, poison glands, and leg attachment sites

ecosystem—all the organisms, plants, and animals in a particular habitat and their interactions

eucalyptus—a flowering tree native to Australia

exoskeleton—a tough, often flexible outer cover and support for many invertebrate animals without backbones

gossamer—fine, see-through material

habitat—the area or type of environment where an organism lives

invertebrate—an animal without an internal backbone

larvae—newly hatched or immature (young) invertebrates, which can look quite different from their adult forms (one is called larva)

mating—the process animals use to transfer sperm for fertilizing eggs and reproducing

metamorphosis—the process by which an invertebrate changes from its newly hatched or immature form into a more mature form; metamorphosis can be incomplete, where the young form looks like a smaller version of the mature form (as in spiders), or complete, where the immature form does not resemble the adult form (the caterpillar and the butterfly)

molting—the process an invertebrate uses to shed its tough exoskeleton and grow a newer, bigger cover as it undergoes metamorphosis

nocturnal—active at night

palp—one of a pair of appendages next to a spider's chelicerae (jaws) used to handle and taste prey, and used by male spiders to transfer sperm in mating; also pedipalp

parasite—an organism that depends on an unrelated host organism for food and/or protection, usually harming the host

pedicel—the narrow "waist" connecting a spider's cephalothorax and abdomen

predator—an animal that kills and then eats other animals

prey—an animal caught and eaten by another animal

sashay—to walk or dance in a sidestepping motion

spinneret—an organ through which silk is produced by spiders; most spiders have three pairs of spinnerets

taxonomy—a system of organizing living things into groups based on shared characteristics, ranging from broad categories like kingdom, phylum, and class to narrower groups like order, family, genus, and individual species

A Few Notes on Poetic Form

The short poems in this collection are written in known verse forms, non-rhyming free verse, and "free rhyme," which is my name for the rhyme schemes I create with no set pattern or an invented pattern.

In many of the poems, I used the following Japanese or Japanese-inspired poetic forms:

Haiku—an ancient, three-line Japanese poem form. In Japanese, the number of syllables in each of the three unrhymed lines should be 5, 7, 5. English language haiku poets use three short lines to refer to a moment in nature, keeping the syllable count to fewer than 17 in all ("The World of Spiders," "Golden Silk Orbweaver," "Diving Bell Spider," "Tiger Wandering Spider," "Spiny Orbweaver Cocoon"). Sometimes I used the haiku form as a stanza, or part of a poem ("Spider Ballooning," "Green Ant-Hunter Spider," "Southern House Spider").

Tanka—an ancient five-line Japanese poem form. In Japanese, the number of syllables in each of the tanka's five lines should be 5, 7, 5, 7, 7. English language tanka poets use five short lines to paint the images they want to share, keeping the syllable count to fewer than 31 syllables in all. I like to use a center "turning" line that can make the first three or last three lines each work as a haiku ("Ogre-Faced Spider," "Spitting Spider," "Long-bodied Cellar Spider").

Dodoitsu—a four-line Japanese poem form from the nineteenth century that could be sung as a folk song and have a funny final line. In Japanese, the number of syllables in each of the dodoitsu's four lines should be 7, 7, 7, 5. English language dodoitsu poets make their fourth line the shortest and keep the syllable count to fewer than 26 in all. ("Mexican Colonial Orbweaver").

Cinquain—a five-line, syllable-counting poem form developed by Adelaide Crapsey, an American poet who studied Japanese poem forms. Cinquain poems follow this pattern: 2 syllables, 4, 6, 8, 2 ("Tarantula").

Other verse forms I used include concrete (or shape) poem, free verse, limerick, rhyming couplet, ballad stanza, poems for two voices, poems based on a songs' rhythm and rhyme scheme, a funny four-line description poem called a clerihew, and one of my very favorites—the double dactyl—which uses a **STRONG**/soft/soft, three-syllable rhythm. To hear this rollicking rhythm, try saying the words **SILK**/ish/ly, **CREEP**/ish/ly from the poem "Appreciate Araneae" out loud.

* "haiku" written in Japanese

Spi-ku Spider Identification

(viewed left to right)

ARANEAE ALL AROUND
desert blond tarantula	*Aphonopelma chalcodes*
ogre-faced spider	*Deinopis spinosa*
common stretch spider	*Tetragnatha extensa*
longbodied cellar spider	*Pholcus phalangioides*
goldenrod crab spider	*Misumena vatia*
black-and-yellow garden spider	*Argiope aurantia*
bolas spider	*Mastophora cornigera*
southern black widow	*Latrodectus mactans*

SPECTACULAR SILK
golden silk orbweaver	*Trichonephila clavipes*
spitting spider	*Scytodes thoracica*
desert blond tarantula	*Aphonopelma chalcodes*

SPIDERS ON THE MOVE
fishing spider (also called dock spider)	*Dolomedes tenebrosus*
common stretch spider	*Tetragnatha extensa*
golden wheel spider	*Carparachne aureoflava*

FOOD PREP, MEALTIME, LEFTOVERS
bolas spider	*Mastophora cornigera*
spitting spider	*Scytodes thoracica*
twig-lining trapdoor spider	*Gaius villosus*
featherlegged orbweaver	*Uloborus glomosus*

WORLDWIDE WEBBERS
black-and-yellow garden spider	*Argiope aurantia*
ogre-faced spider	*Deinopis spinosa*
ray orbweaver	*Wendilgarda clara*

ON THE PROWL
goldenrod crab spider	*Misumena vatia*
woodlouse hunter	*Dysdera crocata*
diving bell spider	*Argyroneta aquatica*

SPIDER FOOLERY
bolas spider	*Mastophora cornigera*
green ant-hunter spider	*Cosmophasis bitaeniata*
Hawaiian happy-face spider	*Theridion grallator*

SPIDEY SENSES
tiger wandering spider	*Cupiennius salei*
white-mustached portia	*Portia labiata*
twig-lining trapdoor spider	*Gaius villosus*

DON'T FEED THE SPIDER-EATERS!
southern house spider	*Kukulcania hibernalis*
longbodied cellar spider	*Pholcus phalangioides*
Goliath bird-eating spider	*Theraphosa blondi*

TRICKY SPIDER ENEMIES
featherlegged orbweaver	*Uloborus glomosus*
ruby-throated hummingbird	*Archilochus colubris*
parasitoid wasp	*Hymenoepimecis argyraphaga*
orbweaver (parasitized)	*Leucauge argyra*
pirate spider	*Ero species*
southern black widow	*Latrodectus mactans*

SPIDER COMES A-COURTING
redback spider	*Latrodectus hasselti*
peacock spider	*Maratus speciosus*
nursery web spider	*Pisaura mirabilis*

SPIDER MAMAS
spiny orbweaver	*Micrathena duodecimspinosa*
fishing spider (also called dock spider)	*Dolomedes tenebrosus*
Australian social crab spider	*Australomisidia ergandros*

SPIDERS IN SPIDERTOWN
Australian social huntsman spider	*Delena cancerides*
Mexican colonial orbweaver	*Metepeira incrassata*
South American social spider	*Anelosimus eximius*

OUR SPIDERFUL WORLD
common stretch spider	*Tetragnatha extensa*
bowl and doily spider	*Frontinella pyramitela*
woodlouse hunter	*Dysdera crocata*
goldenrod crab spider	*Misumena vatia*
southern house spider	*Kukulcania hibernalis*

Spider Hunt!

At night, the wild world of spiders comes alive!

Would you like to visit the dark realm of spiders? Strap on a headlamp and step outside. No headlamp? No problem! Grab a flashlight and a buddy, and let's go...

Move carefully and be sure to watch your step as you head outdoors. With your headlamp on (or your flashlight held next to your head at eye level and pointing forward) sweep your gaze from side to side, about 15 to 20 feet away from you. Check out the ground, grass, shrubs, and tree trunks. Examine inner corners of steps, fences, and porches. Do you see any tiny, greenish lights glowing back at you? If you do, you are looking at your light reflecting off the back of spider eyes! As you walk toward those reflecting eyes you may discover a busy spider weaving a web, prowling its turf, munching a meal, or otherwise hard at work on the Araneae night shift.

Approach slowly. Spiders are super-sensitive to the tiniest changes in their environment and can make a *fast* eight-legged escape.

What do you notice about your spider? Is it as big as your hand, or as small as a pencil eraser? Is its abdomen roundish, or longer than it is wide? Are the abdomen and cephalothorax about the same size or different sizes? How about the legs—long and thin? Or shorter and stouter?

Is your spider weaving a web? Sitting in a web? What shape is the web? What is the web attached to? Or is your spider prowling on the ground or lying in ambush among leaves, with no web at all? Did your spider dash away, or hide?

You can hunt for spiders during the daytime, too—under leaf litter, in the garden, in corners—even *inside*. If you need to relocate one of our hard-working pest-eaters, gently slip a glass or a jar over it that's wide enough not to trap its legs. Slowly slide a postcard or envelope under the glass, letting the spider step onto the paper. Have a close look at your spider. Be sure to keep the paper against the entire rim of the glass when you pick it up to set your spider free.

Have fun recording all of your scientific observations and sketches in a field notebook as you explore the remarkable realm of spiders!

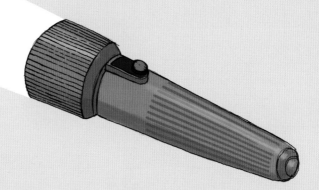

For Further Study

Bradley, Richard A. *Common Spiders of North America*. Oakland: University of California Press, 2013. Sponsored by the American Arachnological Society, this 288-page volume includes meticulous illustrations and detailed descriptions including size ranges, occurrence, and identification tips.

Levi, Herbert W. and Lorna Levi. *Spiders and their Kin*. New York: St. Martin's Press, 2001. An informative, easy-to-read, illustrated guide.

Pringle, Laurence. *Spiders! Strange and Wonderful*. Honesville, PA: Boyds Mills. 2017. Beautifully illustrated, informative 32-page expository nonfiction picture book.

Rayor, Linda. "Spiders: Learning More About Spider Biology." Cornell University. *blogs.cornell.edu/spiders*. Accessed 30 May 2020. A compendium of expert-vetted spider information. Includes an overview of spider biology, materials for teachers, and a bibliography of adult and children's spider reference books.

Smithsonian Center for Learning and Digital Access. "Smithsonian Learning Lab Collection: Smithsonian in Your Classroom: 'Under the Spell of ...Spiders!'" *Smithsonian Learning Lab*, 16 Feb. 2017. *https://learninglab.si.edu/collections/smithsonian-in-your-classroom-under-the-spell-of-spiders/RbTjJfyet3B6ru3d*. Accessed 30 May 2020. Curriculum written for grades 3–8 that begins with an excellent, detailed overview of spiders.

Spiderz Rule. *www.spiderzrule.com*. Accessed 30 May 2020. Extensive, photo-illustrated compendium of spider information for all ages, including taxonomy, anatomy, ecology, and human interest, organized by common group names.

Acknowledgments

I am indebted to Dr. Linda Rayor of Cornell University for inviting me to visit her lab while I was researching *Superlative Birds* during the summer of 2015. Her enthusiasm for arachnid educational outreach is completely infectious. I met amblypygids, tarantulas, and social huntsman spiders of all ages, and this spider book, not previously on my radar, became a must-do. So many thanks to Dr. Rayor and Dr. Cole Gilbert for their generous review of this manuscript.

I would also like to thank Dr. Brian Patrick of the American Arachnological Society for inviting me to join the AAS listserv where a host of arachnologists and enthusiasts answer questions and share fascinating research information. Thank you to Dr. Paula Cushing of the Denver Museum of Nature and Science for her arachnid outreach and manuscript advice.

I am ever grateful to my greater spider clutter, including my critique group, Robert Meganck, Peachtree Publishing, and my family for the support, encouragement, careful attention, and hard work of every kind that contributed immeasurably to bringing this book to life.

—L. B.

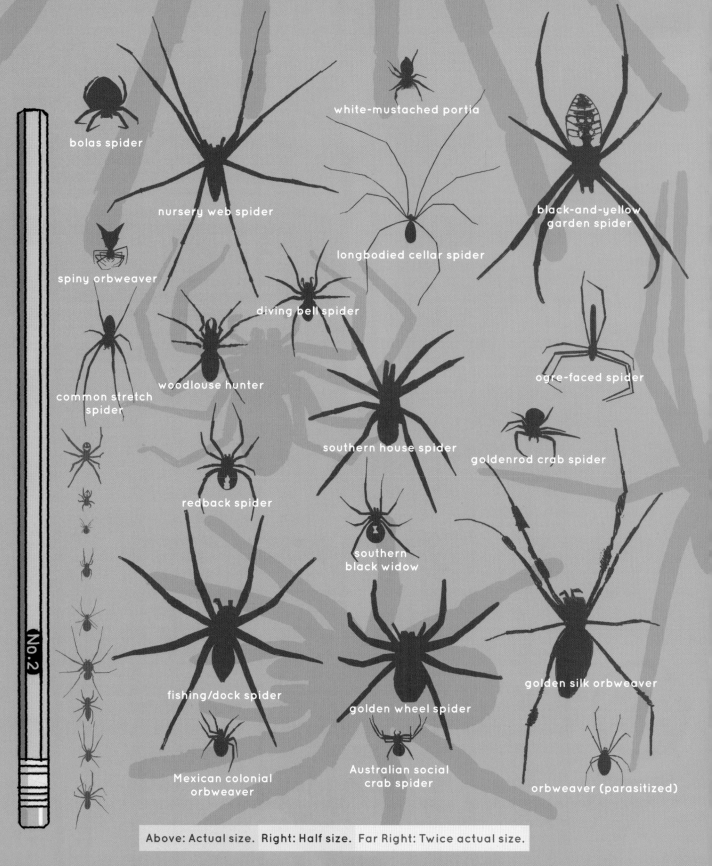

Spi-ku Spiders: Relative Sizes

No.2

bolas spider

nursery web spider

spiny orbweaver

common stretch spider

woodlouse hunter

redback spider

fishing/dock spider

Mexican colonial orbweaver

white-mustached portia

longbodied cellar spider

diving bell spider

southern house spider

southern black widow

golden wheel spider

Australian social crab spider

black-and-yellow garden spider

ogre-faced spider

goldenrod crab spider

golden silk orbweaver

orbweaver (parasitized)

Above: Actual size. Right: Half size. Far Right: Twice actual size.

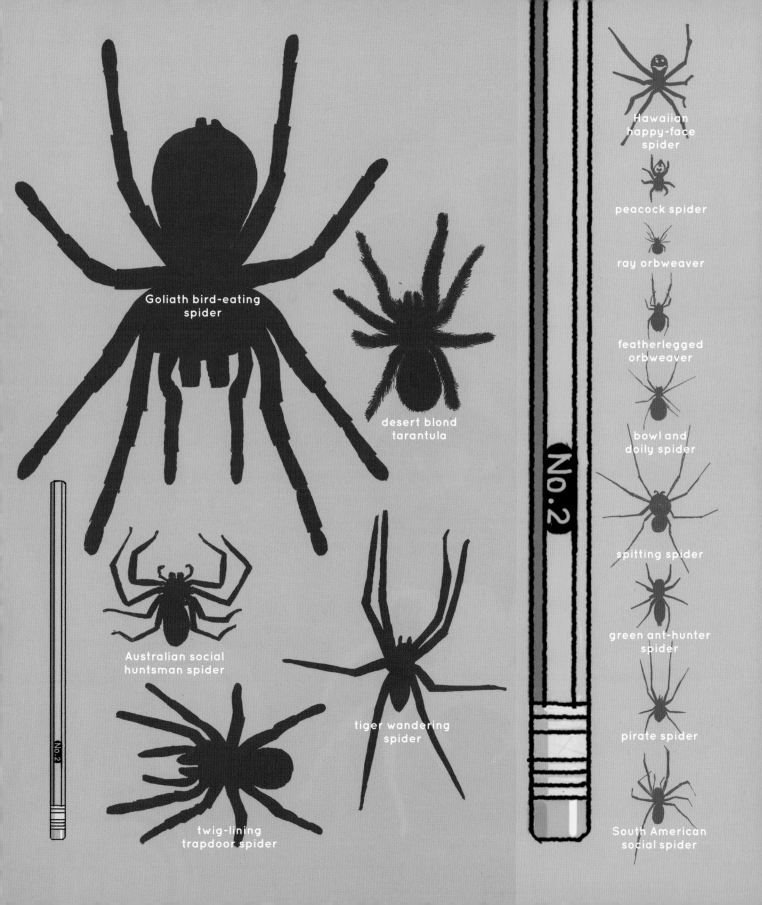

Goliath bird-eating
spider

desert blond
tarantula

Australian social
huntsman spider

tiger wandering
spider

twig-lining
trapdoor spider

No.2

Hawaiian
happy-face
spider

peacock spider

ray orbweaver

featherlegged
orbweaver

bowl and
doily spider

spitting spider

green ant-hunter
spider

pirate spider

South American
social spider

Spi-ku Cover Spiders

spiny orbweaver
(see page 34, "Spider Mamas")

tiger wandering spider
(see page 22, "Spidey Senses")

peacock spider
(see page 33, "Spider Comes A-Courting")

orbweaver (parasitized)
[see page 28, "Tricky Spider Enemies" (part 2)]

woodlouse hunter
(see page 19, "On the Prowl")

longbodied cellar spider
(see page 24, "Don't Feed the Spider Eaters!")

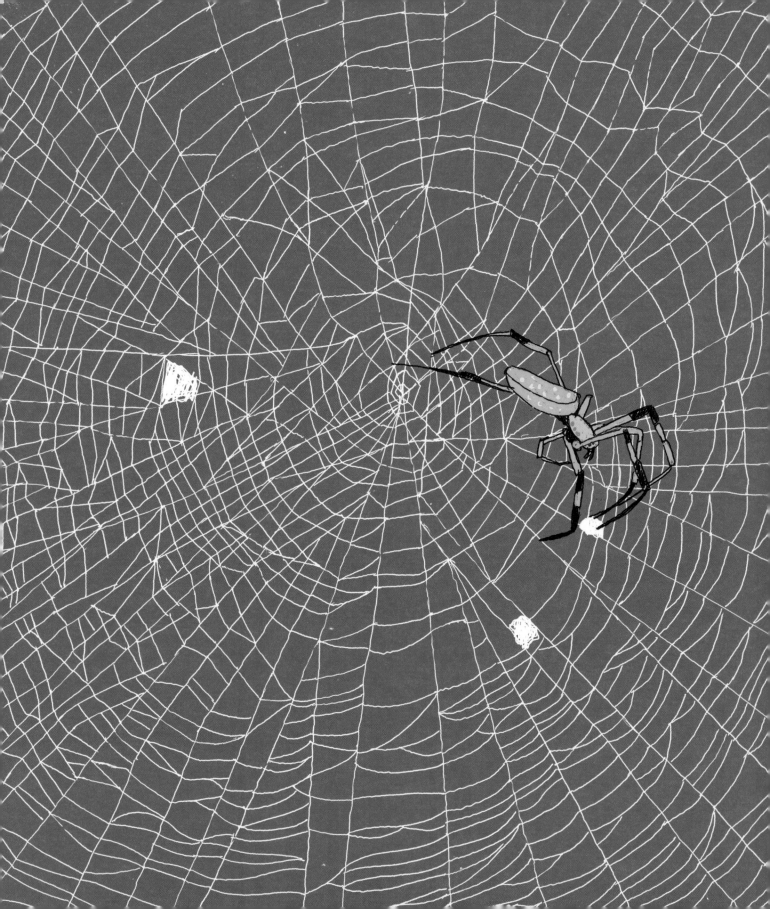